Magic
and
Card Tricks

MARKS &
SPENCER

Magic
and
Card Tricks

Jon Tremaine

Marks and Spencer p.l.c
Baker Street, London, W1U 8EP
www.marksandspencer.com

Copyright © Exclusive Editions 2002

Designed, produced and packaged by
Stonecastle Graphics Limited

Text by Jon Tremaine
Edited by Philip de Ste. Croix
Designed by Paul Turner and Sue Pressley
Photography by Roddy Paine

ISBN 1-84273-853-4

Printed in China

DISCLAIMER
Magic and card tricks are fun and this book will
provide many hours of amusement for magicians
of all ages. Safety is very important – young
children should always be supervised by a
responsible adult when performing tricks involving
sharp objects or scissors. Always read the
instructions carefully. The publisher and their
agents cannot accept liability for loss, damage or
injury however caused.

Contents

Magic Tricks

6

Introduction

Here are some great tricks for an apprentice magician – someone who has just discovered that there is great fun to be had by fooling people. I don't mean making them look foolish. I mean puzzling, amusing and entertaining people with wonderfully subtle conjuring tricks. The joy that you give to those who watch you will only be surpassed by the joy that you will feel when performing the tricks in this book.

Some of the tricks will require you to do a simple bit of "manufacturing" – cutting, gluing – that sort of thing. Don't panic because it is all very simple.

I will not show you how to saw a woman in half or produce a rabbit from a hat. You are not ready for that yet. I will instead show you tricks that you will be able to do almost immediately. I say "almost immediately" because even the simplest trick can only become "magic" if you are prepared to practise it over and over again. Only when it feels natural to you, should you present the mystery to your friends.

8

Be confident. There is a rule in magic that says: "Never tell your audience what you are going to do until you have actually done it!" Stick by this rule and, even if the trick goes wrong, your audience will be none the wiser!

Never repeat a trick straight away. To be forewarned is to be forearmed! If your audience know what you are going to do, there is much more likelihood that they will discover how you do it. Many of your friends will implore you to tell them how your tricks are done. Please don't tell them. We must keep our secrets "secret".

But if tricks must remain secret, you may wonder why I have written this book. Well, new talent has got to come from somewhere. I started by borrowing a book from my local library and just four years later I became a professional magician.

So – be warned – magic is infectious! You could easily catch the bug too!

Good luck and remember – practise hard!

9

The Vanishing Pencil

You threaten to pass a pencil through your hand. Instead it completely vanishes!

2 Lift your right hand with the pencil up to the right side of your head and then bring the point of the pencil down to rest on your palm again.

Count, *"One"*.

Lift your right hand up and down again.

Count, *"Two"*.

1 You will love this cheeky trick! Stand with your left side turned towards the spectator. Hold the pencil in your right hand and extend your left palm in front of you. Hover the point of the pencil above your palm.

Say that on the count of three you will make the pencil pass right through your palm and out the other side.

3 Take your right hand up again, but this time slide the pencil behind your right ear! Bring your right hand down to your palm again.

Count, "*Three!*"

4 The pencil has vanished!

"*Oh, sorry! This is the trick where the pencil disappears!*"

5 It will be ages before the spectator notices that the pencil is stuck behind your ear!

Practise the counting and hand movements until you get a nice easy rhythm going.

Acrobatic Matchbox

A matchbox that is placed on the back of your hand suddenly comes alive. It stands up and, slowly and mysteriously, the drawer rises!

1 We have to make a "special" matchbox. Thread a needle with very thin fishing line (best) or black cotton. Take the drawer out of the matchbox and thread the matchbox cover as shown in the illustration. Tie a substantial knot on one end of the thread and a small safety pin on the other. The thread should be about 50cm (20in) long.

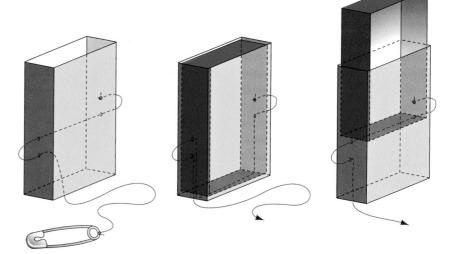

Put the drawer back into the cover (make sure that you put it in the correct way so that it pushes the thread down as illustrated). Attach the pin to the inside of your left jacket or trouser pocket. Put the box in the same pocket. You are ready to perform.

2 Take the box out of your pocket with your left hand and quickly pass it to your right hand. Now place the box on the back of your left hand positioning it near your knuckles.

3 Note how the thread passes down between your left middle and index fingers. Note also that the thread goes to the upper edge of the box. In this position the thread should be taut. Try it out beforehand and shorten it if it is too slack.

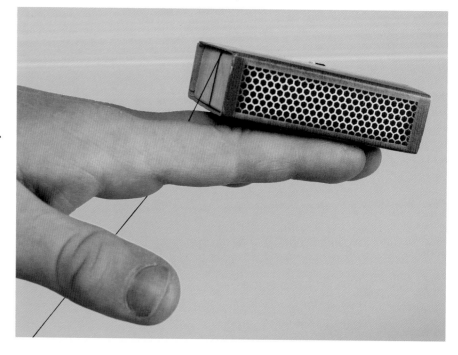

4 If you now slowly and gently move your hand forward the thread will pull the matchbox into an upright position.

Note: Instead of pushing your hand forward, you could try bending your body forward instead. This also causes "pull" on the thread without it being so obvious to onlookers.

13

5 Push further and the drawer will slowly open!

Close the drawer and put the matchbox safely away in your pocket to complete the trick. Mystifying!

Pen-ultimate

You pass a borrowed pen through the centre of a borrowed handkerchief without damaging the handkerchief in any way.

1 Display a handkerchief and then drape it over your left hand and, once your hand is out of sight, open it into a "C" shape – as if you were holding a glass.

2 You now apparently use your right thumb to depress a hole in the centre of the handkerchief by pushing material into the well of your left fist.

3 Actually you push your thumb in sideways so that you drag some of the handkerchief with it – forming a hollow from top to bottom!

Now push your thumb in and out a couple of times from the top downwards – as you should have done in the first place!

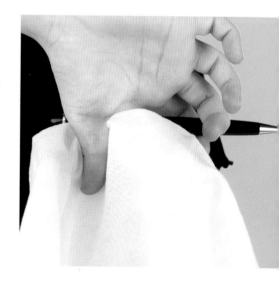

4 Take the pen and slowly push it into your fist. Let it slide through and down the secret hollow.

5 Catch it in your right hand as it comes out at the bottom.

Shake out the handkerchief and show that it has come to no harm.

This is a quick, smart little trick that you can do with all manner of long thin objects, such as pens, pencils and dinner knives and also using borrowed napkins in restaurants.

Have fun!

Walk Through a Postcard

You bet someone that you can make a hole in an ordinary picture postcard and step your body right through it! You then proceed to do just that! Really!

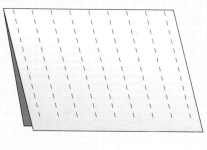

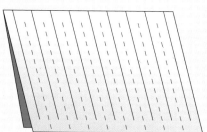

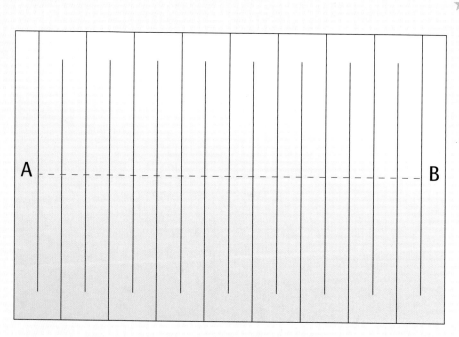

A - B

Well – the trick is in the hole that you cut in the postcard. It is more like an interlinking series of straight cuts that render the small postcard into a very large hoop.

1 Study the illustration well. First fold the postcard in half. From the creased edge make a series of cuts about 1cm (0.5in) apart. Stop each cut about 1cm (0.5in) from the edge of the card.

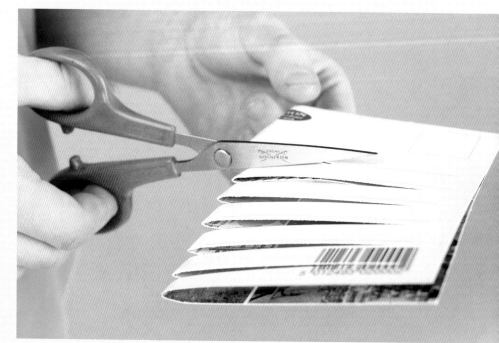

2 Now make a series of cuts from the other side, once more stopping about 1cm (0.5in) before you reach the edge.

Finally cut along the line A-B

3 When you have made all the cuts, carefully open up the card. The hole will get bigger and bigger until you will indeed be able to step right through it.

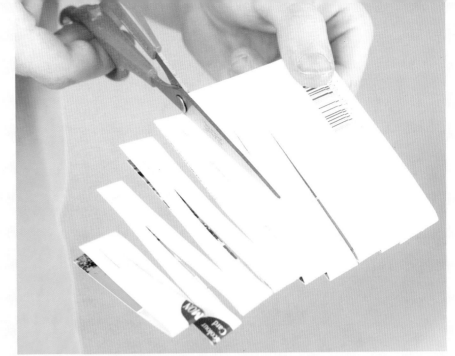

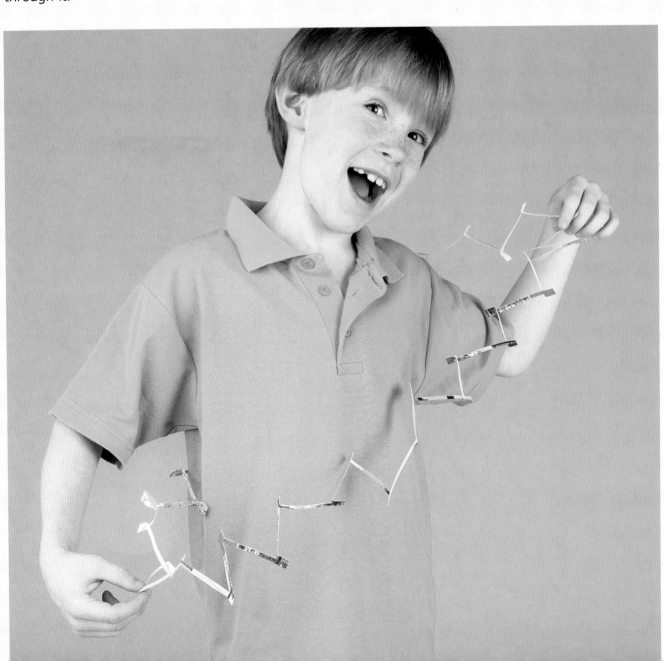

Hoop-la

You and two of your friends have a race to see who can cut around the middle of a paper hoop the quickest. They time you, and you end up as expected with two separate hoops. You give paper hoops and scissors to both friends – challenging them to beat your time. There is great confusion at the end because one finds that he ends up with two paper hoops that are linked together – while the other one ends up with one gigantic hoop, twice the size of the original!

1 Cut lots of strips of newspaper, about 10cm (4in) wide. Join them together with sticky tape. You need three strips – each should be about 2m (6.5ft) long.

Make the hoop that you will use by sticking the two ends together (A). Make sure that you do not get a twist in it.

Put one twist in the second hoop (B) and two twists in the third (C). See diagram on page 21. The hoops are large enough for the twists in the paper to go unnoticed.

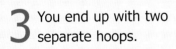 **2** Cut carefully around the centre of your hoop.

3 You end up with two separate hoops.

B

A

C

4 Give scissors and a paper hoop to both your friends, asking them to do exactly as you did.

5 When they finish cutting, they find that things are not quite as they should be!

21

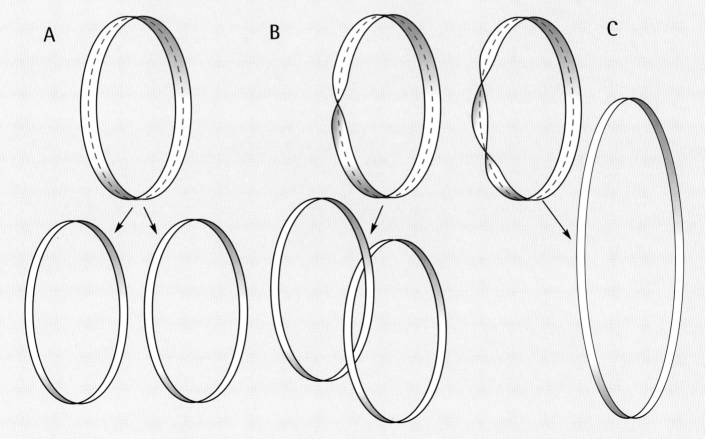

Spooky Laces

Two differently coloured shoelaces are tied into loops and then linked – then one is threaded over a pencil being held tightly at both ends by a spectator. The two laces suddenly change places!

2 After tying the two loops you thread the red one through the yellow one as shown. Note that they are not actually linked together. Thread the red one onto a pencil or wand, again as illustrated.

3 Have a spectator hold each end of the pencil.

Say that you will try to get the red shoelace off the pencil even though he is holding both ends of it. That's impossible!

1 You will love doing this crazy self-working trick. I didn't believe this until I tried it! Nor will you!

Look at the diagram carefully. Our shoelaces are red and yellow.

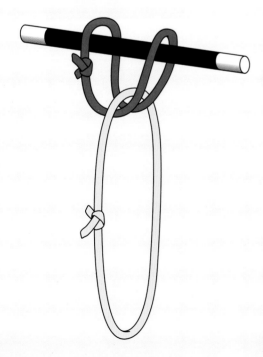

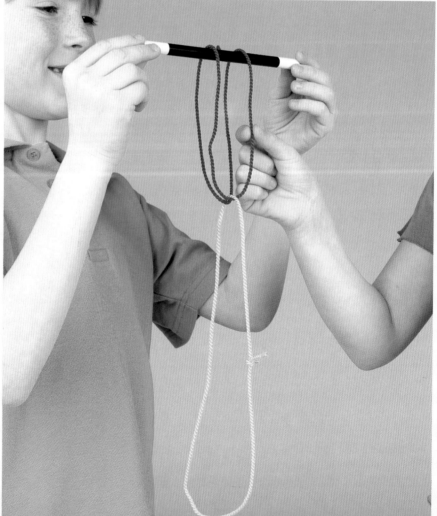

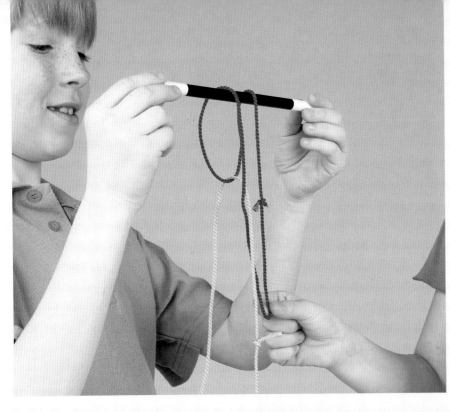

4 Prove the impossibility of your claim by tugging on the yellow lace a few times. Then quickly grab the red lace at the point shown and pull sharply downwards.

5 The two shoelaces instantly change places – the red is now shown to be hanging from the yellow one – and the yellow lace is where the red one was a moment ago, securely trapped by the pencil that the spectator is holding!

Quickly repeat the trick by pulling on the yellow lace in the same place. The two laces will immediately return to their original positions!

Note: The trick works just as well with ribbon, wool, string or rope – so don't worry if you can't lay your hands on differently coloured shoelaces.

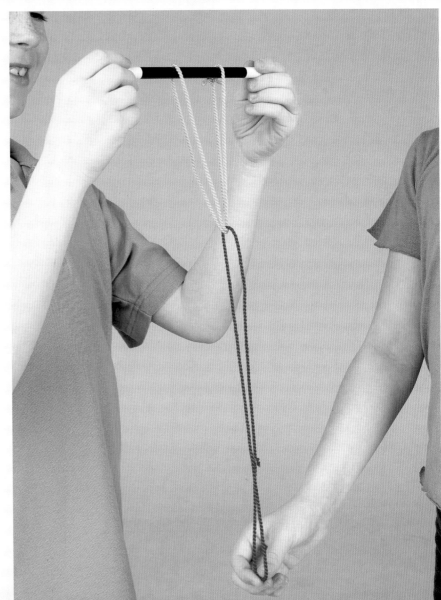

Heads or Tails?

You give a friend a coin and turn your back so that you cannot see. He then spins the coin on a hard tabletop. When it settles, you name which side is uppermost – amazing!

1 Take a round coin and with a small metal nailfile make a nick in the top edge so that a little of the metal sticks out.

2 Turn your back so that you cannot see, and get a spectator to spin the coin on a hard polished tabletop and listen carefully.

3 As the spinning stops and the coin comes to rest upon the table, it will make a noticeably different sound depending upon which way up it lands. This is our secret.

4 You can repeat the trick several times without fear that your method will be discovered.

25

Figure Out - Figure Eight

A length of cord is tied into a figure of eight. You remove the centre loop without untying the knots!

You'll need about 1 metre (3ft) of cord for this one.

1 First form a large loop in the middle.

2 Next tie the ends of the cord together with a couple of knots.

3 Have the spectator add as many more knots to yours as she wishes.

6 The loop becomes just another knot in the bunch that's already there and your spectator won't be able to see the wood for the trees!

4 Challenge your friend to remove the centre loop without undoing the knots. She is bound to fail – the whole thing's impossible!

5 You take the figure of eight behind your back and, as soon as everything is out of sight, slide the centre loop down until it joins the other knots.

Pull sharply on the sides of the loop.

Houdini Beads

Three large wooden beads are threaded and tied onto two lengths of cord. The spectator holds both ends of the cords yet you still magically manage to remove the beads without cutting the cord. Everything may be examined.

The beads I use are about 3cm (a little over 1in) long and the two lengths of cord are both about 1 metre (3ft) long. There is a little preparation to do before you demonstrate the trick

1 Fold both cords in half. Push one cord through one of the beads until the centre loop emerges from the other end. Hook the centre of the other cord through this loop as shown.

2 Hold onto the bead and carefully pull on the first cord until the secret link becomes hidden inside the bead. It now looks like two separate cords are passing right through the bead!

To perform the trick, start threading two ends of the cords through another bead and get a spectator to thread the third bead on the other two ends. Be careful not to pull your secret join from its hiding place.

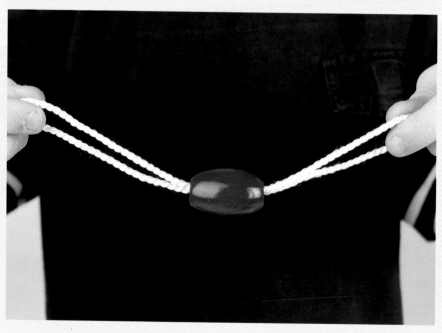

3 Give the "necklace" to the spectator to hold loosely between her hands.

4 Ask her to give you one cord from each end (it doesn't matter which ones).

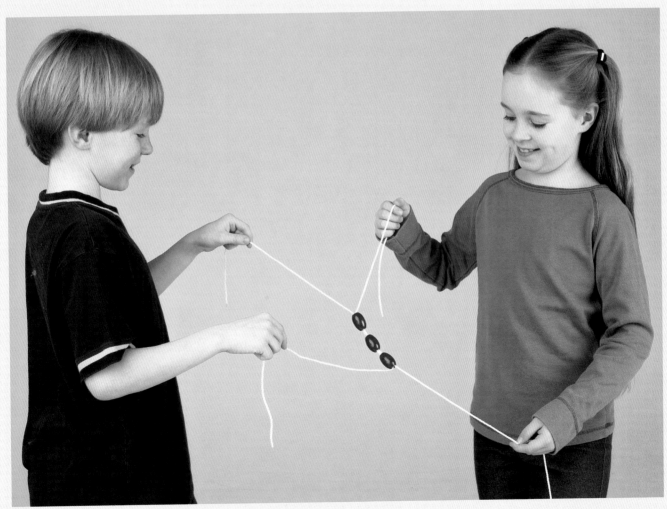

5 Take them and tie a simple knot – then give the ends back to her.

6 In this action she takes the ends back in the opposite hands that they came from.

30

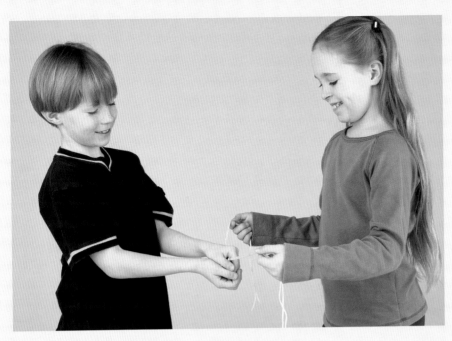

7 Cover the beads with both of your hands and start sliding the beads backward and forward until they come free.

8 She finds that she is still holding the two cords and there is no clue as to how the three beads escaped!

Note: If you cannot lay your hands on any large beads, you will find that cotton reels will do just as well.

Dynamic Dominoes

Placing a sealed envelope on the table, you then ask your friend to lay out a set of dominoes, placing matching spots together, as if she were actually playing a game. When she has finished, she opens the envelope. You have correctly forecast the two numbers at each end of the domino layout!

2 Start by putting the sealed prediction on the table. Don't say what is in the envelope.

1 She only plays with 27 dominoes instead of 28. You secretly steal a domino beforehand (not a double)!

Let's assume it is a 3/5. Write on a piece of paper:

"Your end numbers will be 3 and 5!"

Seal it in the envelope.

3 When your friend has laid out all the remaining dominoes, the end spots will always match the numbers on your stolen domino.

4 Have her open the envelope and read your amazing prediction!

Note: If you want to do the trick again, you must pinch another domino and secretly put back the first one as you help to shuffle up the dominoes!

33

Your end numbers will be 3 and 5!

The Hypnotized Coin

You balance a coin on end on your outstretched fingers. After a few seconds the coin slowly and mysteriously glides downward until it lies flat upon your fingers. No trace of any method can be found. It looks really spooky!

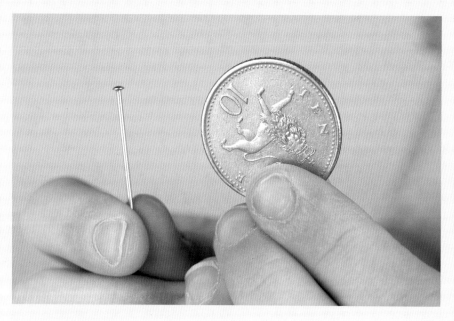

1 Our secret is a common or garden pin!

2 Hide the pin behind the coin as you show it to the spectator.

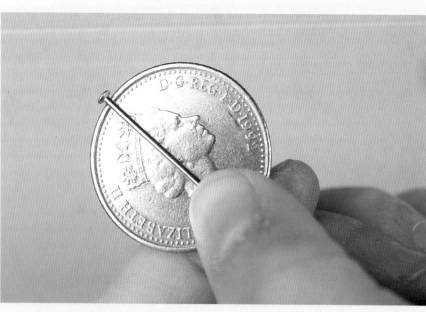

3 Place the coin in the position shown and slip the head of the pin down between your middle and index fingers until you can grip it.

6 Practise this until you learn to control the rate of its descent. The pin now lies between your fingers and is hidden beneath the coin.

7 Open your fingers slightly and let the pin fall unseen onto the floor. Nobody will notice it – the evidence has vanished!

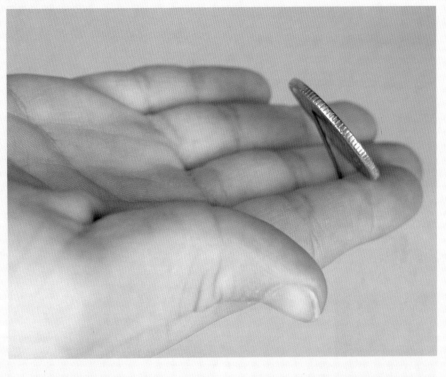

4 Let the coin lean on the pin and it will remain upright.

5 Gradually ease your grip on the pinhead and the coin will slowly descend onto your palm.

35

The Disappearing Pen

You display a ballpoint pen on your hand, then cover it with a handkerchief. You shake out the handkerchief and the pen has vanished.
You retrieve it from your pocket!

You need:
Two identical pens
50cm (20in) of cord elastic
A safety pin
A handkerchief
(You'll need to wear a jacket to perform this trick)

36

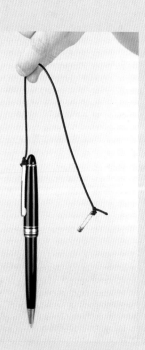

1 Put one pen in your jacket pocket. Tie one end of the elastic to the clip of the other pen. Fix the safety pin to the other end.

2 Fix the safety pin to the cloth near the armhole and drop the pen into the right sleeve of your jacket. Adjust the length of the elastic so that the pen will hang just out of sight up your sleeve.

3 With your left hand secretly pull the pen out of your sleeve until your right fingers can hold it. Make sure that the elastic is hidden from view.

4 Cover the pen with the handkerchief.

5 Run your fingers around it so that the handkerchief takes on the shape of the pen.

6 Let go of your grip on the pen and the elastic will pull it up your sleeve out of sight. Keep holding the handkerchief as if the pen was still there. It certainly looks as if it is.

7 Take your time – then shake out the handkerchief to reveal that the pen has disappeared.

8 Show that your hands are empty and then remove the duplicate pen from your pocket! How did you do that?

Brow Beating

You press a small coin onto the centre of your forehead. It sticks there. It drops off when requested and you catch it in your hand. Push the coin onto a friend's brow. It sticks too – but when she requests it to drop off, the coin vanishes!

This is quite spooky and relies on the sense of touch. If you have ever worn a hat, you will know what I mean. It feels as if it is still on your head even after you have taken it off, doesn't it?

1 Take any small coin and press it firmly onto your forehead. The natural oils in your skin will keep the coin in place. Just frown or raise your eyebrows when you want it to drop off at your command. Catch the coin.

2 Now press the coin firmly onto your friend's forehead – but immediately (and secretly) take the coin away again. Drop the hand that holds the coin casually to your side.

She will still "feel" the sensation of having a coin stuck to her forehead.

3 Tell her to command the coin to drop off. She will screw her face up into all sorts of contortions before she finally realizes that the coin has vanished into thin air!

Coin in the Slot

In this smart trick you make a coin penetrate through the centre of a borrowed handkerchief.

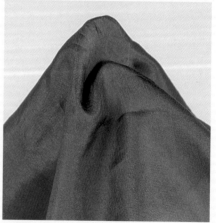

This pretty "quickie" is very easy to do.

1 Hold the coin in your right hand and the handkerchief in your left hand.

2 Drape the handkerchief over the coin so that it is positioned at the centre of the cloth.

3 Grip a little of the cloth between the coin and your right thumb.

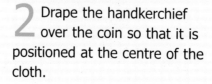

4 Pull the front part of the handkerchief up and over to show that the coin is still there. Now secretly get hold of the other part of the handkerchief and let both parts of the handkerchief drop forward as you cover the coin again. The coin is now secretly on the outside!

5 Change your grip and twist the lower part of the handkerchief around.

6 Now mysteriously start to pluck the coin slowly out. It looks just as if you are pulling the coin through the material!

Shake out the handkerchief to show that it is undamaged.

The Dancing Pencil

Having dropped a pencil into an empty bottle, you make a magic pass and the pencil starts to dance and jig about in the bottle. It finally jumps right out of the bottle and you hand it out for examination!

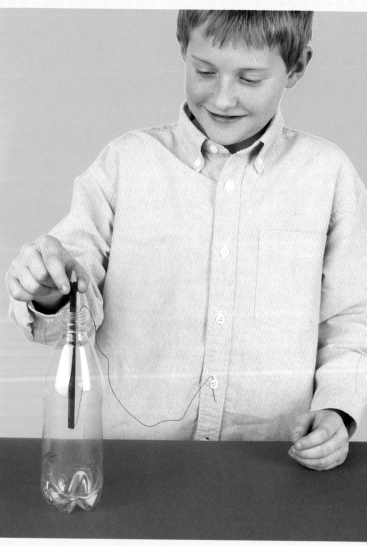

1 It's our old friend the secret thread again! Attach one end to the bottom of the pencil with a small dab of Blutak. The other end is tied to your shirt button.

2 Drop the pencil into the bottle. The threaded end goes to the bottom as shown in the photograph. Any small movement on your part will cause the pencil to jig about in an eerie way inside the bottle.

3 Finish by moving back sharply. Catch the pencil as it comes clear out of the bottle. Push the hand holding the pencil forward a little and the thread will become detached from the pencil and drop down to hang unnoticed from your shirt button (try to choose a colour that matches your shirt). Secretly peel off the Blutak before handing out the dancing pencil to be examined by your startled friends!

Fantastic Elastic

A rubber band that encircles your first and middle fingers instantly and visibly jumps to encircle your other two fingers.

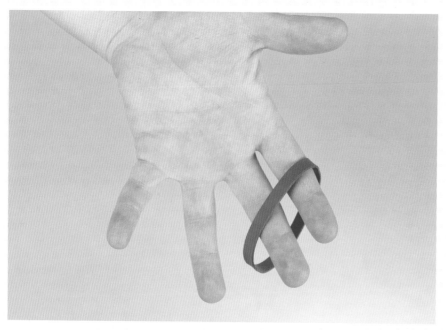

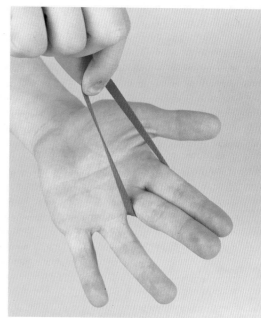

1 Put your first and second fingers into the elastic band. Your palm is facing upwards.

2 Lift up the centre of the band – stretch it and release it, snapping the band to show that it really encircles your two fingers.

3 Lift the centre once more and secretly insert all four fingers into the loop.

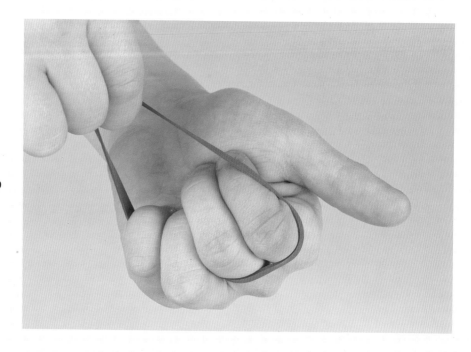

44

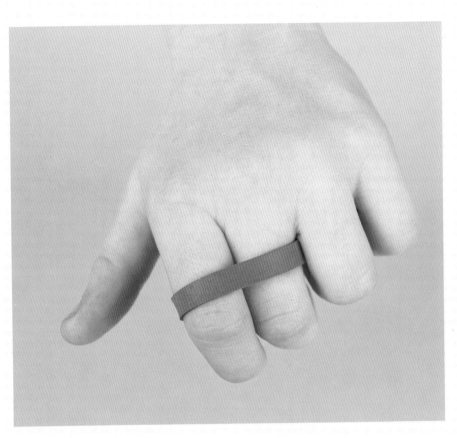

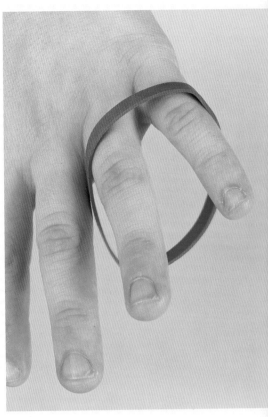

4 At the same time quickly turn your fist back upwards.

5 Open your fist quickly and spread your fingers. The elastic band jumps to your other two fingers.

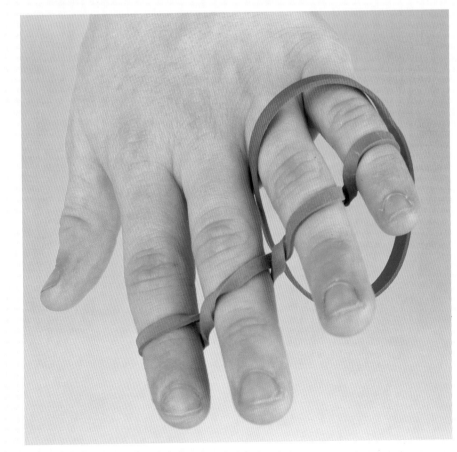

6 You could make things even more impressive by taking a second elastic band and twisting it around all four fingers as shown in the photograph. Follow the instructions as before and the first band will still jump across.

Hanky-Panky

You drape a handkerchief over your left fist – then push a coin into its centre. You shake out the handkerchief and the coin has disappeared!

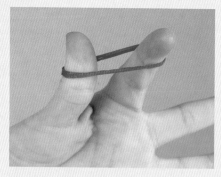

1 A small elastic band makes the trick possible. Secretly wrap the band around your left index finger and thumb as shown in the picture.

Drape the handkerchief over your left hand and immediately bring the hand into an upright position so that your elasticated thumb and finger are directly beneath the centre of the handkerchief.

2 Pull the finger and thumb apart – stretching the band. With your right hand push a coin into the centre of the handkerchief. It goes through the centre of the hidden band taking a little of the material with it.

3 Remove your left finger and thumb and the elastic will snap shut trapping the coin in a little secret pocket.

4 Shake out the handkerchief and the coin has vanished!

Which Coin?

You borrow two coins and end up
winning both of them!

2 The spectator peers closely
at the coins and you say...

*"Which one of these two coins
did you give me?"*

She will say...

"I gave you both of them!"

This is a cheeky swindle and
should be done after you have
dazzled everyone with a couple
of stunning tricks.

1 Borrow two coins from a
member of the audience.
Then display them – one on
each palm. Close your fingers –
open them – close them – open
them again. You then say...

*"Look closely and carefully at
the two coins now".*

3 Quickly put the two coins into your pocket and say...

"That's very kind of you. Thank you very much!"

Run for it!!!

Note: As we magicians always cheat fairly, you will give her the two coins back, won't you?!

Anti-Gravity Glasses

Two glasses are placed on a book. The book is turned upside down. The glasses defy gravity by not falling off!

You need:
A book
Two tumblers (practise with plastic ones)
A handkerchief with a wide hem
Two small beads
A length of cotton

1 Link the two beads together with cotton to make the little gimmick illustrated here. The space between the beads should be the same as the width of your thumb.

2 Feed the gimmick into the hem of the handkerchief (there is always an opening at one end).

3 Fold the handkerchief lengthways a few times making sure that the secret bead gimmick ends up on the top surface. Wrap it around the book.

51

4 Place the two tumblers on the handkerchief so that a bead goes inside the rim of each tumbler.

5 Press your thumb between the glasses and pick up the book. The pressure from your thumb will be enough to anchor the two tumblers and you can safely turn your hand and the book over.

6 The glasses will not fall off until you ease your thumb pressure!

Cut and Restored String

You display a piece of string and then cut it into two equal pieces. You tie the two pieces together. The knot disappears and the string is shown to be whole again!

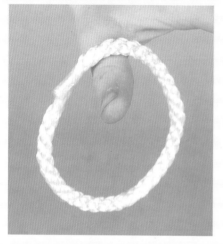

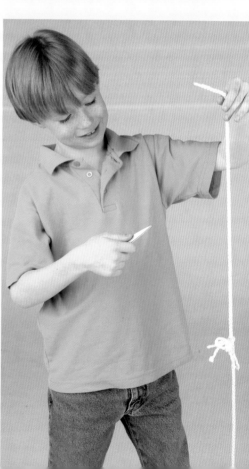

1 First you must fashion a small loop from a 10cm (4in) length of string. Join the two ends with sticky tape.

2 The string that you will apparently cut should be about 1 metre (3ft) long. Secretly thread the loop on to the centre of the string. You are ready to begin.

Display the string. The loop at the top looks as if it is part of the long string.

3 Cut through the loop – then tie the ends together around the centre of the string.

4 It will look as if you have merely tied the two separate halves together.

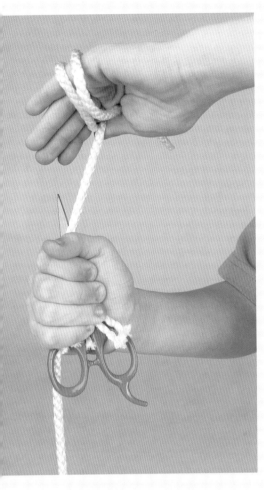

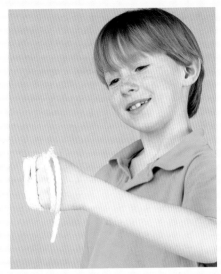

Note: You can use the same piece of string for several performances before it gets too short to handle comfortably.

53

5 Keep the scissors in your right hand. Your left hand holds one end of the string and your right hand starts to wrap the rest of the string around your left hand.

6 The fake knot will secretly slide off and can be disposed of in your pocket when you put the scissors away!

7 Say a few magic words over your left hand and then slowly unravel the string to show that it is fully restored.

Linking Mints

Two separate hollow mints are shown. You close your hand over them. When you open your hand, they have become magically linked together!

1 Snap a mint in half as cleanly as you can. Moisten the ends and push them together again after threading them through another whole mint.

2 The broken halves will meld together quite well. The joins will be almost invisible.

3 Sit at a table for this trick. Conceal the linked mints in your left hand. Place two whole mints on the table in front of you.

54

4 Slide the mints towards you with your right hand as if you were picking them up. Instead, let them drop unseen onto your lap. Keep your right fist closed as if it still held the mints.

Pretend to pass the mints into your left hand. Show that your right hand is now empty.

5 Slowly and dramatically open your left hand to show that the two mints have somehow magically been linked together.

Afterwards – eat the evidence! You're in the clear!

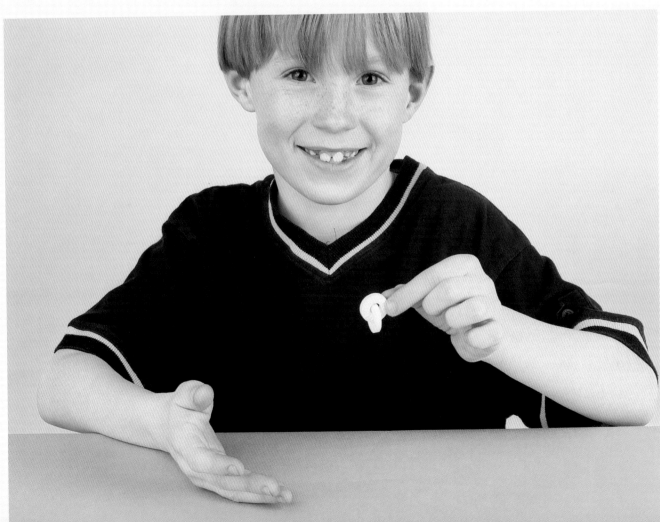

Together Apart

You openly link two safety pins together and then you grip them between the finger and thumb of each hand. A sharp pull and, voilà! The pins are now unlinked but they are still unopened!

There is a knack to this although, if you follow the photographs carefully, it will be a piece of cake to perform.

1 Get two safety pins (the larger the better). Link them together as shown. Make sure that the opening and solid joins to the pinheads are correctly placed. This is important.

56

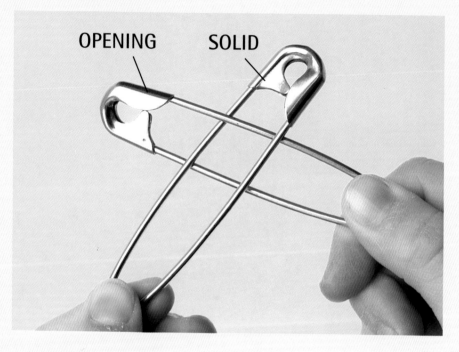

OPENING   SOLID

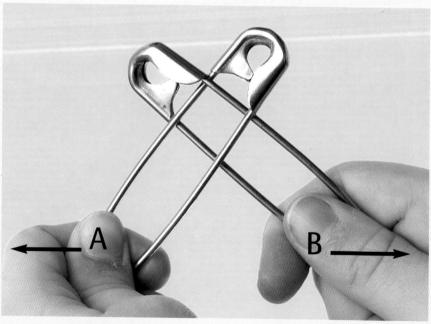

A   B

2 Your left hand grips a pin at point "A". Your right hand grips the other pin at point "B".

Pull sharply in opposite directions.

57

3 You will be amazed to find that the two pins have come apart yet both pins are still securely closed.

I A F Y D S T T A !

What's that, you say? If at first you don't succeed, try, try again!

Simple Thimble

A thimble, displayed on the tip of your index finger repeatedly vanishes and reappears.

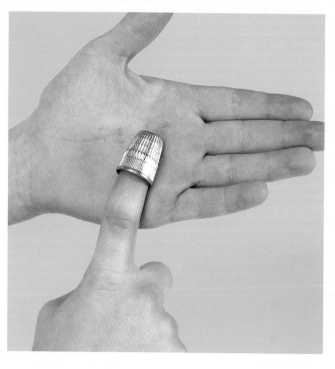

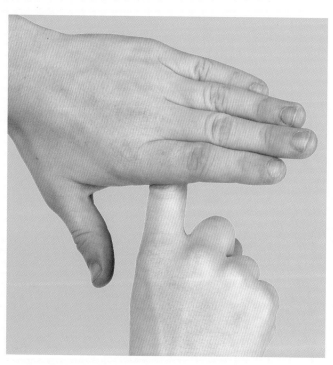

58

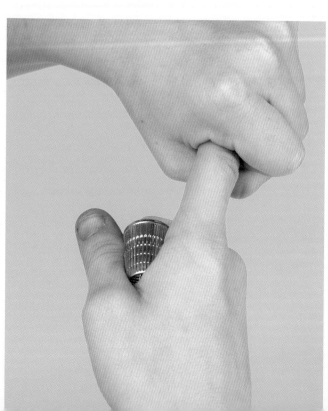

1 Stick a thimble on the tip of your right index finger.

2 Shield the thimble from view with your left fingers.

3 As soon as the thimble is hidden from the spectator's view, bend your finger inwards.

Grip the thimble between the fork of your index finger and thumb. Immediately shoot the finger forward again and grip it with your left fingers. Pull your left fist off the finger as if you have just removed the thimble with it.

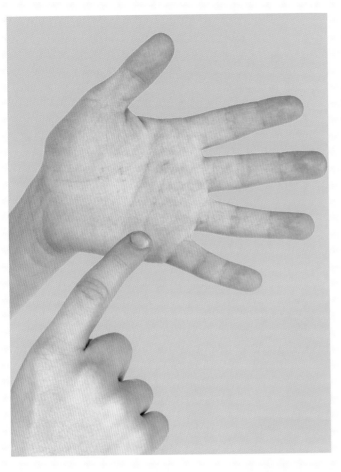

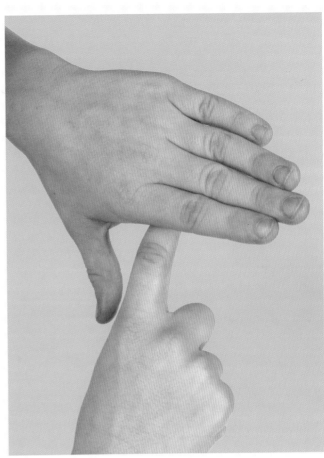

4 Open your left fist. The thimble has vanished.

5 To make it reappear just hold your left hand palm away from the audience. Delve behind it with your right hand. Once it is out of view, bend your index finger to get the thimble from its hiding place and back on its tip again.

6 Bring your right hand into view again with the thimble resplendently displayed on the end of your index finger.

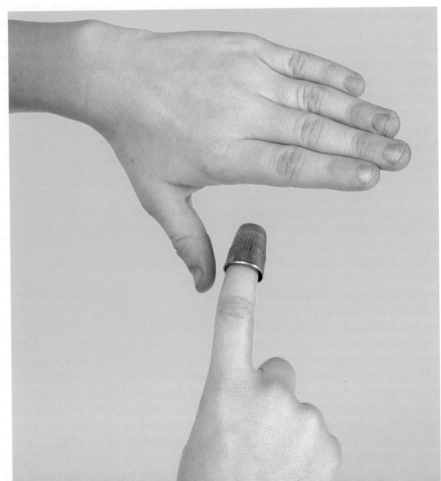

The Wax Works

You hand out a set of five differently coloured wax crayons. One is chosen while your back is turned. Without seeing any of the crayons, you instantly reveal the correct colour!

This is really cheeky!

1 Give all the crayons to a spectator, then turn your back so you cannot see him.

2 Instruct him to choose any crayon and place it in your hand (which is behind your back), then hide the other four from view.

3 When he has done that, you turn around to face him, still holding the crayon behind your back so that you cannot see it.

4 Secretly scrape the end of the crayon with your fingernail so that a minute sliver of wax gets lodged beneath it.

5 Keep the hand that holds the crayon behind your back. Bring the other hand that has scraped the crayon forward to press to your fevered brow as you apparently concentrate on reading his mind! Casually spot the colour of the wax scraping beneath your nail in the process!

After a few moments of "concentration" tell him what colour crayon he is thinking of! Reveal the crayon from behind your back to prove your genius!

Prediction

You write a secret number on one side of a piece of paper. The spectator calls out four different numbers that range from 1 to 16 selected from a grid that you show him. These numbers are added together. Their total is the same as the number that you previously wrote on the other side of the paper!

1 The joy of this little gem is that it works automatically. The number that you write down is always **34**.

On the other side of the paper write out the numbers 1 to 16 like this:

1 2 3 4

5 6 7 8

9 10 11 12

13 14 15 16

Ask him to call out any of the numbers. Say he says: **11**. Cross it through both ways – then draw a circle round it.

1 2 3 4

5 6 7 8

9 10 (11) 12

13 14 15 16

Ask him to call out any other number that has not been struck through. Say he says: **5**.
Cross it through both ways and draw a circle round it...

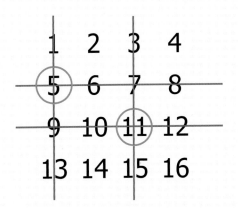

Ask for another number not yet struck through, say: **4**. Strike it through and encircle it.

This leaves **14**. Draw a circle round it.

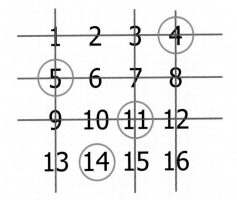

Add together the encircled numbers: 4 + 5 + 11 + 14 = 34

2 Turn over the paper to show that you have already predicted his total. Yes! It will always be **34**!

Walking the Tightrope

You balance a table tennis ball on a piece of cord.
Then you cause it to run backwards and forwards –
performing an impossible tightrope act!

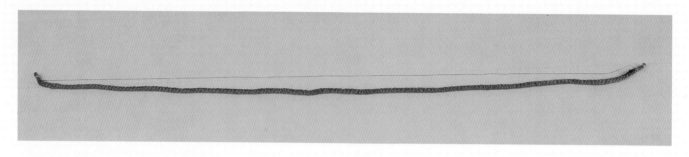

1 Tie a thin length of cotton or
fishing line to both ends of a piece
of cord as illustrated. It will not be
visible to the audience.

2 Lay the cord on the table and place the ball
on its centre. Pick up the two ends of the
cord and insert a finger between the thread and
cord at each end.

3 Lift the cord into the air and the ball will come too. The channel that is formed between the cord and the secret thread will support it. It looks as if the ball is balancing on the cord.

4 By tilting the cord slightly to and fro, you can make the ball run up and down the cord in a truly mysterious manner. It must be magic!

65

Card Tricks

Introduction

These card tricks are all very easy to do – some of them require no skill at all! I have purposely chosen tricks that I know you will be able to perform. Although no finger skills are required, you will need to develop skill in the performance of the tricks. This can only come with practice. If you are prepared to practise the "handling" of the cards and your "patter" as you talk to the audience until you can do it almost without thinking, you will be rewarded with a variety of spectacular card tricks that would grace any magician's act.

You will need two packs of cards. Both packs should have backs with white borders. Get one with a geometric back design that looks the same whichever way round you hold it. The other pack should have a picture back or non-geometric design on its back. I'll tell you why later!

An old geometrical deck will also be useful for making up certain "special" cards that you will need – so don't throw your old cards away!

So – for the price of just a couple of packs of cards – you are about to enter the wonderful world of card magic.

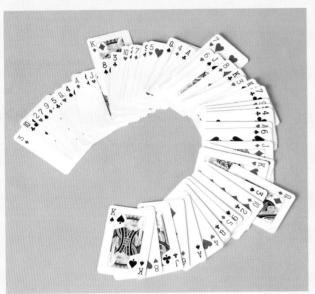

Card Words

There are a few special words that
card magicians use:

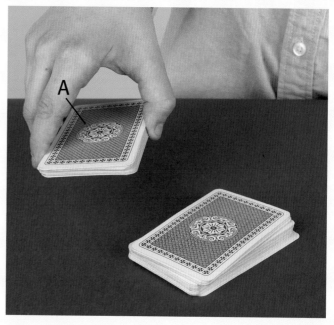

CUTTING

1 Cutting is a simple way of changing the order
of the cards in a deck. Take some of the
cards (A) off the top of the deck and put them
down to one side.

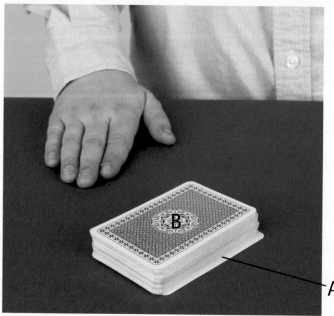

SHUFFLING

To shuffle is to change the order of all the cards
in the deck. Hold the deck in one hand and take
up a few cards with the other. Put the cards back
into the pack, a few at a time in different places,
so the order of the cards is changed. Repeat this
until all the cards have been shuffled together.

2 To complete the cut, pick up the bottom half of
the deck (B) and put it on top of the rest (A).

Geometrical Back   "One Way" Back

THREE GOLDEN RULES

• Keep our secrets secret! Magicians do not tell anyone how they do their tricks.

• Practise your tricks until they become second nature to you. Then – and only then – perform them for your friends.

• Make sure that your hands and fingernails are always clean. People will be watching your hands all the time, so give them something pleasant to look at!

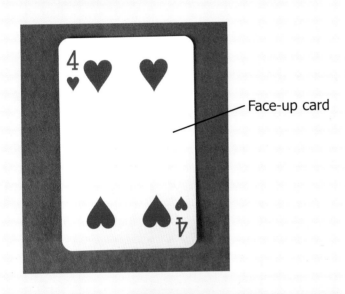

Face-up card

Face-down card

71

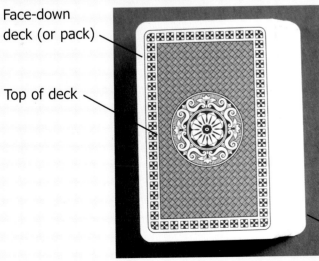

Face-down deck (or pack)

Top of deck

Bottom of deck

Face-up deck

One-Way Street

Your friend chooses a card – puts it back in the pack – then shuffles the pack herself thoroughly. You are still able to find her card.

We use the deck with the picture back for this trick. Magicians call this a "one-way deck". Before you perform the trick make sure that all the pictures on the backs of the cards are *facing the same way*. This is our secret.

1 Spread the cards between your hands so that your friend may remove one. Fan them if you can. While she is concentrating on looking at and remembering the name of her card, you close the fan or spread and secretly turn the pack round.

2 Now when she puts her card back in the deck, it will be the only one that has an upside-down picture!

3 To reveal her card, hold the deck up at eye level and run through the cards with the faces towards her. Ask her to think hard when she sees her card. In this way you are cleverly able to look at the backs of the cards without her becoming suspicious.

4 As soon as you see the
one upside-down card,
take it out and display it with
a flourish!

The Key Card

You find the chosen card under what appear to be "impossible" conditions.

The "key card" principle is quite well known but will still fool people if you present it with enough confidence.

Secretly remember the bottom card of the deck after you have shuffled it. We will assume that it is the 8♥.

1 Place the deck on the table. Get the spectator to lift off about half of the deck and shuffle these cards.

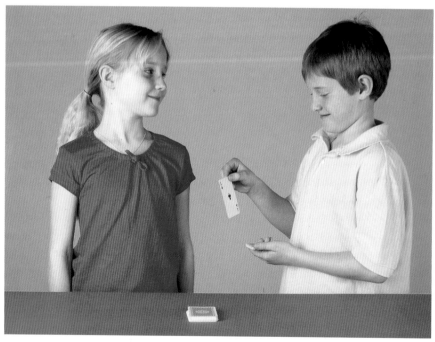

2 When he is happy that the cards are well mixed, he must look at and remember the card that he has shuffled to the top.

3 He must then place the cards back on top of the lower half that he left on the table.

You cut and complete the cut. This brings your 8♥ (key card) to the centre of the deck and directly on top of his "remembered" card!

4 You merely have to look through the cards and remove the one that is directly beneath the 8♥. It will be the chosen card.

Roll Call

You find all 13 cards of one suit one at a time and in sequence. This nice little trick will create quite a problem for the spectator when he tries to duplicate what you have done.

1 Remove all 13 cards of one suit and secretly arrange them as follows:

3, 8, 7, Ace, Queen, 6, 4, 2, Jack, King, 10, 9, 5. (The 5 will be the bottom card).

Casually show the cards to your spectator then turn them face downwards. Tell him that all 13 cards will now answer to their names.

76

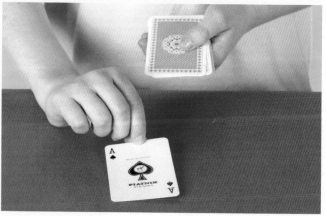

2 Spell out the word ACE by taking one card from the top of the packet and transferring it to the bottom ("A") – then a second ("C") – then a third ("E").

3 Turn the next (4th) card face up and place it on the table. It will be the Ace!

Spell out the word TWO in the same way with the remaining 12 cards – transferring a card for each letter from the top to the bottom of the packet.

Turn the next card face up and deal it onto the table. It will be the Two!

4 Continue spelling out the rest of the cards in the same way.

All the cards will make their appearances on cue.

5 Even when you are down to just two cards, the Queen will appear on request leaving you holding a single card – the King!

The 21 Card Trick

You tell the spectator what card he is thinking of even though he doesn't touch the card.

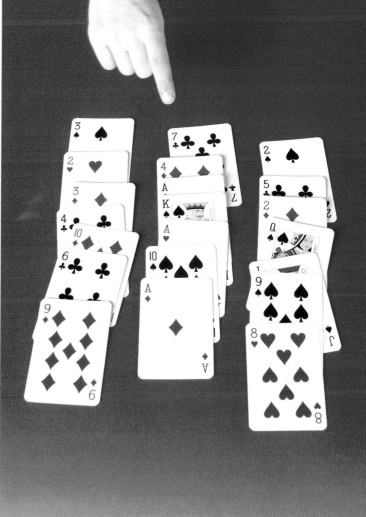

1 This is an automatic trick based on a mathematical principle. You deal three cards face up in a line – then another three cards that overlap the first three. Keep adding a card to each pile until you have dealt out 21 cards into three rows – each containing seven face-up cards.

2 Ask the spectator to think of any one of the 21 cards that he can see and just indicate which of the three rows his choice is in without revealing to you which particular card he has chosen.

3 Gather up the three piles, making sure that the pile that he has indicated is sandwiched between the other two.

Deal out your three rows again and ask him to indicate which row his card is in now. Collect up the three piles with his selected line of cards sandwiched between the other two again.

Repeat the procedure a third time and collect them in again. His chosen card will now be the eleventh card from the top. Believe me!

4 Deal the three face-up rows out again. His chosen card will now be the middle card in the middle row.

Ask him to think intently of his card. Reach down and dramatically point to and then remove the correct card!

The Q Trick

The cards are laid out in the shape of a letter "Q". A spectator looks at the layout and thinks of a card while you are out of the room. You tell him which one it is without even having to see the cards again!

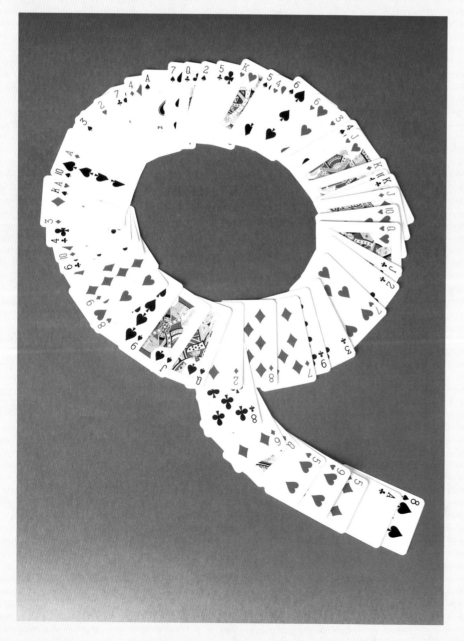

1 Once again subtle mathematics come to our aid. The number of cards in the tail of the "Q" layout gives us a clue to the position of the card he is thinking of.

Look at the photograph. There are eight cards in the tail.

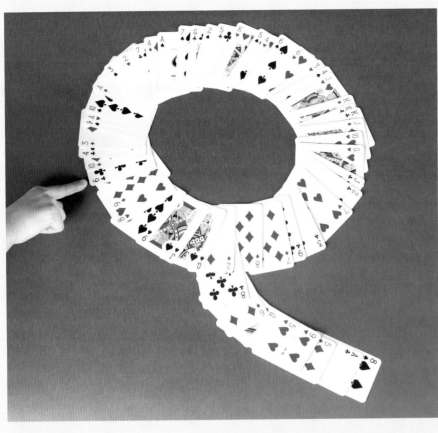

2 Tell the spectator to *think* of a number between 10 and 30. For example we will assume that he thinks of 15. Beginning at the end of the tail he must silently count along the tail and then clockwise around the left side of the circle until he reaches the 15th card. Then, counting this last card as "1", he must count back anti-clockwise (bypassing the tail) until he reaches a count of 15. He must remember this card. In our example it will be the Q♥.

3 Now try the experiment with any other number between 10 and 30. You still end up on the Q♥! Eight cards to the right of the tail!

If there were only five cards in the tail, the chosen card would be the fifth one to the right of the tail. So we see that by varying the number of cards in the tail, we can alter the card on which the spectator's choice will fall and so can repeat the trick without the method becoming apparent.

As you lay the cards out in the Q shape, you simply have to note how many cards are in the tail and then remember the card that lies that number of places to the right of the tail. It's as easy as that!

81

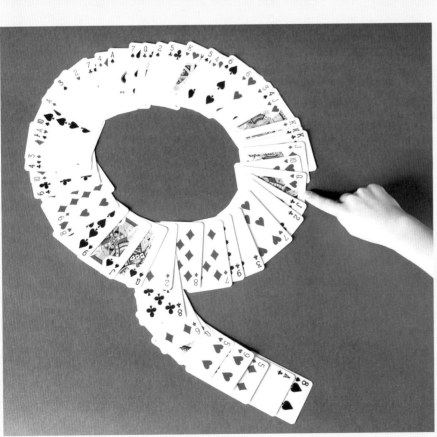

The Balancing Card

You stand a playing card on its edge and, as if that wasn't enough, you proceed to balance a wineglass on top of it!

1 You make a special "hinge" card. Take one of the Jokers and slice it in half lengthways. Fix one half to the back of a playing card with a sticky-tape hinge.

2 The tape should be on the inside so that (to a casual glance) the back of the card appears normal when the flap is closed. Put this special card in the middle of your deck of cards before you start. Have a small wineglass handy.

82

3 Take the card out of the deck and try to balance it on its short edge. Fail miserably a couple of times to make it look difficult. Allow it to fall (face up) on the table. On your third attempt secretly open the flap. Take your hands away and – hey presto – the card balances!

4 Quickly pick up the wineglass and balance it on top of the playing card. The secret flap makes this possible. Remove the glass after a few seconds and put the balancing card back in the pack, folding up the flap as you do so.

If the spectator wants to try – just give him a different card!

Warning: The trick is best viewed from the front so watch your angles – overhead and side views are definitely out!

Note: Save all your old packs of cards. They will be useful as a source of obtaining duplicate cards and for making up "special" cards like this which may be required for certain tricks.

Find the Lady

A Queen (the lady) is clearly shown to be the centre card in a fan of three. They are laid face down on the table. The Queen changes into an entirely different card. She is then shown to have jumped into your pocket!

You will need two identical Queens and three other contrasting cards. Put one Queen in your pocket.

1 Cut the other Queen to the shape shown and stick it onto the face of one of the other cards.

2 Take the other two cards and, holding them together as if they were only one card, place them over the half-Queen. Show the cards as illustrated in the photograph. It looks as if the Queen is the centre one of three.

3 Turn the cards face down and deal them side by side onto the table from left to right.

4 Ask a spectator to point to the Queen. He will point to the centre one.

Pick up the *right-hand* card and use it to scoop up the left-hand "gimmicked" card so that when you turn them face up, the right-hand card covers up the stuck-on half-Queen.

Seeing this, the spectator will be convinced that he has chosen the correct one that is still lying face down in the middle.

86

5 Get him to turn it face upwards. He finds it to be a totally different card. Reach into your pocket and remove the other Queen!

Out of Thin Air

Two cards are shown and put back in the centre of the deck. The deck is tossed onto the table but somehow the two selected cards remain in your hand.

This is dead cheeky! It relies on the fact that most people cannot remember more than one thing at a time.

1 Prepare by placing the Jack♥ on top and the Jack♠ on the bottom of the pack. Take the deck out of its case and with the faces of the cards towards you look for and remove the Jack♦ and the Jack♣. Place them face up on the table. Do not name them.

2 Pick up the two Jacks from the table and openly stick them back into the deck, losing them somewhere in the centre of the pile.

3 Square the deck up. Now grip the cards fairly loosely and throw the cards onto the table.

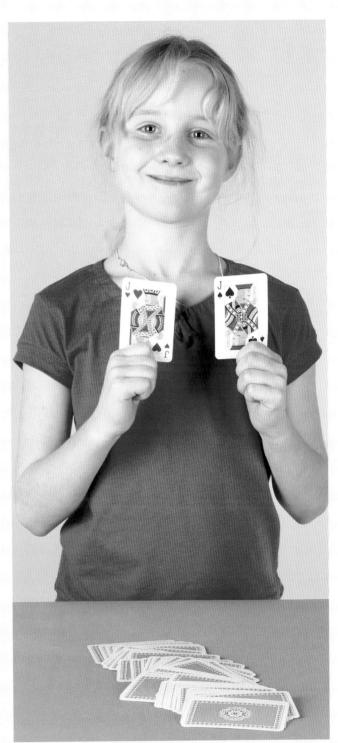

4 With practice you will find that the top and bottom cards of the deck will stick between your thumb and index finger while the rest will fall to the table.

5 These two cards will be the two Jacks (J♥ and J♠) that you previously placed there. They are so similar in appearance to the two that you buried in the deck that the fact that they are not actually the same two cards will not be noticed. Well hardly ever!

Hugard's Odd Even Trick

You deal out two apparently even piles of cards. By placing one extra card on the pile that the spectator chooses you magically turn it into a pile containing (not an odd) but an even number of cards, while the other pile now contains an odd number of cards instead of an even number of cards!

 You bamboozle the spectator with words! Have him place his hands on the table as if he was playing a piano.

90

Take two cards – show them – and wedge them in the gap between the ring and little fingers of his left hand as you say:
"Two cards – a pair – even."

Take another two cards and after showing them wedge them between his left middle and ring fingers. Say:
"Two cards – a pair – even."

Take two more cards. Stick them between his left middle and index fingers.
"Two cards – a pair – even."

Take one card. Place it between his left thumb and index finger. Say:
"One card – single – odd."

Continue four more times – taking two cards each time. Stick them in the corresponding four gaps between the fingers and thumb of his right hand. Note that two cards go between his thumb and index finger this time – not one as before.

As you place each pair say:
"Two cards – a pair – even."

2 Now take a pair of cards away from him and place them on the table about 15cm (6in) apart. Say:
"Two cards - a pair - even."

Take another two and place these on top of the first two.
"Two cards - a pair - even."

Continue taking away pairs and assembling two piles on the table – each time saying:
"Two cards - a pair - even."

It's called brainwashing! Now take the single remaining card.
"We have two piles with an even number of cards in each. Right?"

They all agree. They are wrong – but they will agree nevertheless!
"So - if I place this last single card on one of the piles it will make that pile odd - right?"

3 Place the card on the pile that they choose.
"I will now transfer one card from the pile that you have just made 'odd' onto the 'even' pile. It will go by magic – so don't expect to see it go!"

Make a magic pass – then pick up the pile that you placed the odd card on. Count them in two's:
"Two, and two, and two and two - even!"

Count the other pile:
"Two, and two, and two and one - odd!"
It certainly is!

KAAKAAKK

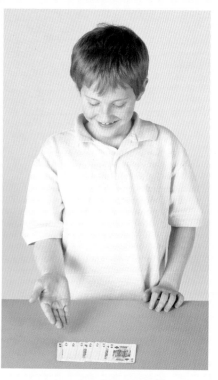

A pile of eight cards consisting of the four Aces and four Kings is held. The first card is transferred to the bottom of the packet and the next one dealt face up on the table. It is an Ace. The next card is placed on the bottom and the following card dealt onto the table. It is a King. You continue to deal out the cards in this way.

They alternate as they appear:
Ace – King – Ace – King – Ace – King – Ace – King
Challenge your friend to duplicate this stunt.

92

1 Secretly arrange the cards so that from the top the order reads...King, Ace, Ace, King, Ace, Ace, King, King.

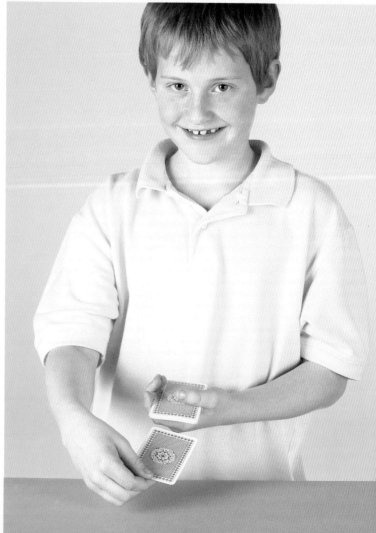

2 Hold the packet face down in your left hand. Remove the top card and place it on the bottom of the packet without showing its face.

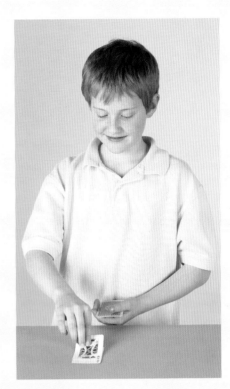

3 Deal the next card face up onto the table. It is an Ace.

4 Transfer the next card from the top to the bottom.

5 Deal the next card face up onto the table. It is a King.

6 Carry on with this procedure and the cards will appear alternately Ace, King, Ace, King, Ace, King, Ace, King.

It looks very simple to do but unless your friends stumble upon the secret starting order, they will get in an awful mess trying to copy you.

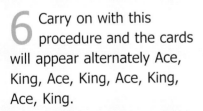

The Pre-arranged Deck

If you could only memorize the order of all 52 cards in the deck when they are apparently arranged randomly it would be possible to do some amazing tricks, wouldn't it?

It is easier than you think. If you can remember a simple sentence plus one extra word you have got it made!

The sentence to remember is: *"Eight Kings threatened to save ninety-five ladies for one sick Knave."*

Look at the sentence:
Eight Kings threatened to save ninety-five ladies for one sick Knave.
8   King   3   10   2   7   9   5 Queen   4   Ace   6   Jack

This "sentence order" is repeated four times.

The word to remember is "Chased."

The four suits are alternated throughout the pack and the word "chased" reminds us of the order like this:

C	Ha	Se	D
Clubs	Hearts	Spades	Diamonds
♣	♥	♠	♦

1 The photograph shows you the completed layout.

Note: You can give the deck as many single complete cuts as you wish without disturbing the set up. Complete cuts will only change the starting point of the 52-card sequence.

3 Cut the pack again. Look at the bottom card. We'll assume it is the 8♥. The top card will be the K♠!

Play about with the arranged pack until you become familiar with it. Your efforts will be rewarded.

2 Cut the pack a few times, then look at the card that is now on the top. Let's assume it is the 2♣. In our sentence the word "to" (2) is followed by the word "save" (7). **Chased** tells us that the next card suit is Hearts – so the second card will be the 7♥! Followed by the 9♠ – then the 5♦ – and so on.

The following pages show you some super tricks that you can perform with this pre-arranged deck.

Think of Your Card

You can instantly name the card
that a spectator is thinking of!

1 Spread your pre-arranged
deck of cards so that the
spectator can choose and
remove one.

2 Take all the cards above
the point of her selection
and put them under the
other half.

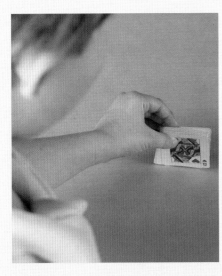

3 Place the deck on the table, *casually* looking at the bottom card as you do so.

4 Mentally advance one card in your sequence and you know what card she has selected.

Examples:

If the bottom card is now the Q♥ – she will have chosen the 4♠.
If the bottom card is now the 10♣ – her card will be the 2♥.

Important: Replace her card on the top of the deck when you have finished the trick. This will preserve your pre-arrangement.

One in the Middle

The spectator makes as many complete cuts of the deck as she wishes. When she is satisfied, you instantly name the middle card in the deck. You count down to the 26th card to prove it!

1 As we have already seen, complete cuts of the pack do not disturb our sequence. They only change the starting point of the 52-card cycle.

2 Our clue to the identity of the middle card is again obtained from a secret glance at the bottom card of the deck once her sequence of cuts has been completed.

3 The middle card will be the same colour and value as the bottom card but will be of the other suit of that colour.

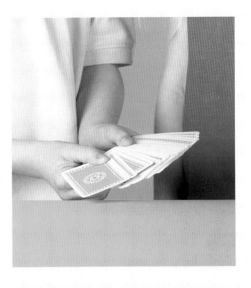

Examples:

If the bottom card is the K♠ – the middle card will be the K♣
If the bottom card is the K♥ – the middle card will be the K♦
If the bottom card is the 2♦ – the middle card will be the 2♥
If the bottom card is the 2♣ – the middle card will be the 2♠

What could be easier?

Triple Choice

Three people choose cards. They are put back into the deck, which is then cut a number of times. You look through the deck and unfailingly locate all three!

It's our pre-arranged deck again!

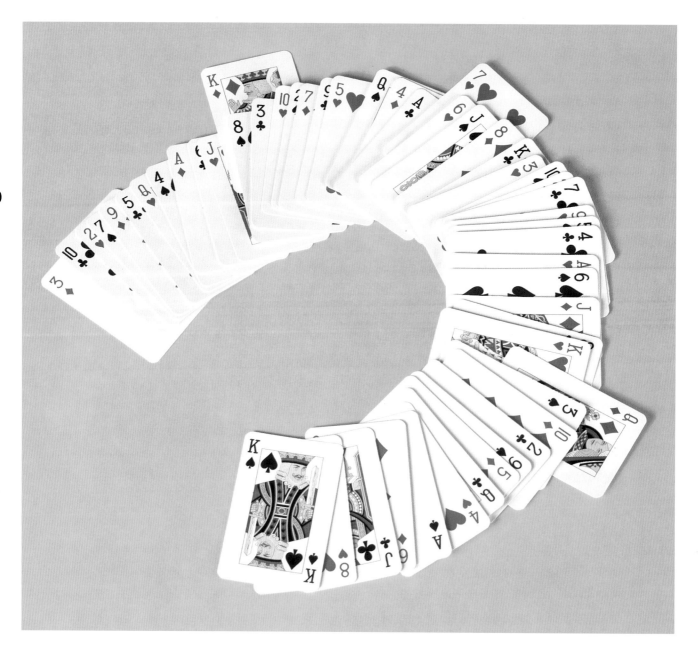

1 Spread the cards and have three people each remove a card from *different* parts of the deck. Stress that they must remember their choices.

Have the three cards returned to the deck in separate sections of the pack but make sure that they are not replaced in the same place from which they were originally taken.

Give the deck three or four complete cuts and then give the spectators the option to do further complete cuts if they wish.

2 Look through the cards with the faces turned towards yourself. The three chosen cards will stick out like a sore thumb because they will be breaking the sequence of your pre-arranged deck as shown in the picture (opposite page). Remove the three cards and place them face downward on the table.

3 Ask the three spectators to name their cards aloud. Turn over the three tabled cards with a flourish.

You've done it! Three for the price of one!

Behind My Back

The spectator chooses a card while your back is turned. You name her card in a most startling manner!

This trick with our pre-arranged deck is a stunner! Timing is everything!

1 Take the deck out of the card case and, holding the cards behind your back, spread them between your hands for a selection to be made. As the spectator removes a card, you will be able to feel the position that it is removed from. Cut the pack at this point taking the top half to the bottom.

2 Ask the spectator to remember her card and then replace it somewhere in the middle of the deck. Your back is still turned while this happens. Turn round to face her once her card is pushed flush with the rest of the cards.

3 Immediately hand her the deck with the request that she shuffle it thoroughly and then replace all the cards back in the card case and put everything in her pocket out of sight.

This is the moment that you *casually* glimpse the bottom card. The card that she chose will be the next one in the sequence. For example, if the bottom card was the 10♠ – then the one that she chose would be the 2♦!

She shuffles, re-cases the deck and hides it from sight as requested. There should be no way that you could know the name of her card. But you are a magician, aren't you?

After much "browbeating" and "concentration", tell her the name of her card. She will be astounded.

Note: She has destroyed all traces of your method and every shred of evidence by thoroughly shuffling the pack. How is that for cheek?!

Four to One Against

A spectator thinks of one of five cards then shuffles them. You unfailingly find her card!

This is the last of our pre-arranged deck tricks.

1 Put the deck on the table and give it a couple of complete cuts. Invite the spectator to cut a few times until she is happy.

2 She must then take the top card – look at it – remember it – and place it face downwards on the table.

3 Instruct her to cut the deck *once* more and then deal four cards face downwards on top of her chosen card. The rest of the deck is then put to one side.

She is instructed to pick up the packet of five cards and thoroughly shuffle them so that you could not possibly know which one she chose.

4 You take the five cards and look through them. There will be two cards of the same suit and one of them will not fit our sequence.

Take it out and place it face down on the table. Have her name her card.

Turn the card face up. Wow!

105

Moving Day

A row of cards is laid face down on the table. While your back is turned, the spectator moves any number of cards from one end of the line to the other. When you turn around, you immediately turn one card face up. Its value tells you the number of cards that he transferred. You can repeat the feat as often as you like.

1 Take out any Jack, 10, 9, 8, 7, 6, 5, 4, 3, 2, and Ace. The suits do not matter.

2 Lay them *face down* in a row, from left to right, in the same order. Do not show the faces to the spectator.

3 Ask the spectator to move any number of cards (one at a time) from the right end to the left end and remember how many cards he moved. To illustrate what you want him to do, you move *six* cards in this manner from the right end to the left end. Your first "key number" will be *6*.

Turn your back so you cannot see what he does and turn back only when he tells you that he has finished the task.

4 Look him in the eyes as if reading his mind, then reach down and turn up the sixth card from the left. It will signify the number of cards that he has moved. If it is a two, he has moved two cards. If it's a four, he has moved four cards! Turn it face down again.

Add this number to your first key number and you will have a new key number. We will assume that it was a two. 2 + 6 = 8. Eight is your new key number.

Repeat the trick and this time turn up the eighth card from the left. You are right again.

You can repeat the trick as often as you wish but three times should be enough to have the spectator tearing his hair out!

Note: If, after a couple of turns, your key number amounts to more than 11, just subtract 11 from the total and continue with the new lower key number.

If you turn up the Jack, it will signify that the crafty spectator is trying to catch you out by not moving any cards!

The Circus Card Trick

The spectator is so convinced that you will not find her card that she is prepared to put her shirt on it! She loses! Don't take her money – you may be a cheat but, remember, you must always cheat fairly!

1 Secretly look at and remember the bottom card before you start. Let's say it is the 6♣.

2 Spread the cards for the spectator to choose one, remove and remember it.

108

3 Close the spread of cards.

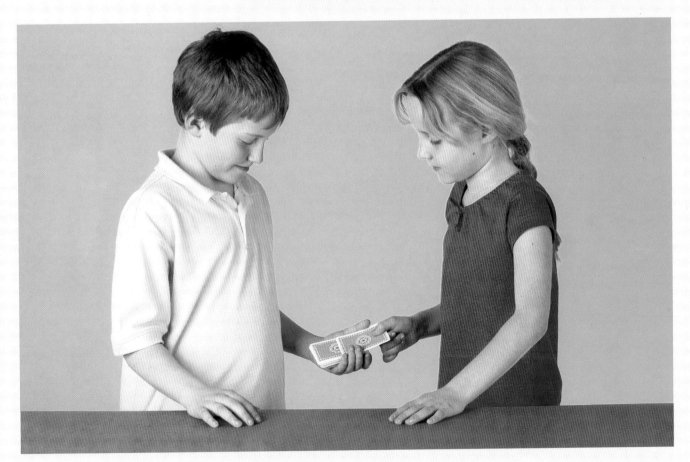

4 Have her replace her card on the top of the pack. Cut the deck and complete the cut. This brings your "key card" (6♣) directly above her card. Keep giving the deck complete cuts. Allow her to cut as well, if she wishes.

5 Slowly start dealing the cards face up onto the table. When you spot your key card, you know that the next card will be the one that she chose. Remember it but ignore it!

6 Keep dealing until you have dealt another five or six cards further on.

7 Take the next card and, without turning it up, feel its face with your fingers. Hesitate a little. Feel the card again and replace it on top of the deck. Then say:

"Yes – I think I've got it – I bet you that the next card that I turn over will be your card!"

She has already seen you deal her card five or six cards earlier so she will be keen to accept your bet.

8 Reach down and turn over her card – the one already on the table next to the 6♣. She'll be speechless!

Me and My Shadow

You choose a card from one deck – she chooses a card from another. Inexplicably you both choose the same card!

A key card and a "little white lie" help you here! Stand opposite your friend with the two decks of cards on the table. Ask her to pick up one of the decks – you pick up the other.

"Please try to do exactly as I do."

1 Shuffle your cards – she shuffles hers.

112

2 Swap decks as you say:

"I've shuffled mine and you have shuffled yours. Now you take my cards and I'll take yours. We have mixed them up so neither of us can possibly know the order of the cards. Right?'

Secretly glimpse the bottom card of the deck as you hand over your cards! Remember it.

3 *"Look through the cards – remove any one – remember it – square up the deck – place your card on top – and finally cut the cards so that your card is lost somewhere in the deck."*

4 You carry out all these actions and she follows suit. Don't bother trying to remember the card that you placed on top. You won't be seeing it again!

113

5 Swap packs again.

6 *"Look through the cards and remove the card that you have just chosen – and place it face down on the table. I will do the same but please let me put my card down first!"*

114

7 Look through the cards for your "key" card and *remove the one that is beneath it*. Place it face down on the table. She does the same.

8 *"I'll count to three and we must turn our cards face upwards at the same time. Ready? 1, 2, 3!"*

The cards are identical! What a coincidence!

What a Turn Up!

The spectator's card is found reversed in the middle of the deck under impossible conditions.

1 Secretly turn the bottom card of the deck face up before you begin.

2 Spread the cards so that the spectator can select a card. Be careful not to flash the bottom card that you have reversed.

3 Square up the deck and hold it in your left hand. Ask him to look at his card to make sure that he remembers its name.

As he is looking at it, *very casually* turn your left wrist over – flipping the pack and bringing the bottom card to the top. Don't make a meal of it – just do it. Your action will not be noticed.

4 Keeping the cards tightly squared up, get the spectator to insert his card into the deck and push it all the way in. He will not notice that the deck is in fact upside down with only a single face-down card on the top.

"I will now attempt to find your card without even looking at the pack."

5 Hold the deck behind your back and quickly flip the top card over! Now the only reversed card in the deck will be the one that he chose.

6 Bring the deck forward and spread it out face up on the table. Spread them so that he can see that there is just one card reversed in the middle of the deck.

7 Ask him to name the card that he chose and then turn over the reversed card with a flourish. Watch his face when he realizes that it is the card that he chose!

Magic Mind

You claim to be able to name every card in a thoroughly shuffled deck of cards without even looking at them! Then you prove it!

1 You use a "key" card that you must first mark on the back with a minute pencil dot in the top left- and bottom right-hand corners. We will assume that it is the 7♥.

2 Make your outrageous claim and give the deck to the spectator for a thorough shuffling. Emphasize that she must keep the faces of the cards turned away from you at all times.

118

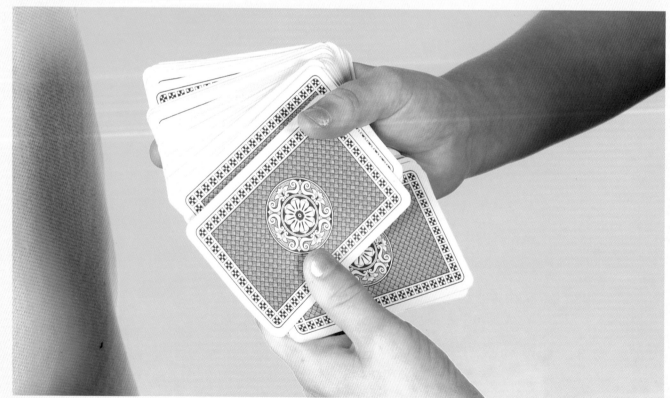

3 Take back the deck being careful to keep it face downwards so that it is obvious that you cannot see any of the cards. Spread them slightly so that you can locate the pencil dot in the top left-hand corner of the key card. Casually cut the pack to bring it to the top.

Place the deck behind your back and flip your key card (7♥) face upwards.
Say: *"The Seven of Hearts!"*

4 Bring the pack forward and hold it vertically in front of you with the 7♥ facing the spectator.

5 The bottom card of the deck is now facing you and cannot be seen by the spectator. Let's say it is the 9♣. Put the deck behind your back again and transfer the 9♣ to the top – over the 7♥.

Say: *'The Nine of Clubs!'*

Bring the pack forward again at arm's length. She sees the 9♣.

A new card is now staring you in the face. Remember it and transfer it to the top as soon as the cards are behind your back again. Name the card and bring the deck forward again.

Just name about a dozen cards in this way – no more. That should be quite enough to convince the spectator that you are a person with very special powers!

119

Odds and Evens

Two friends each take half of the deck. They each choose a card from one another's half – bury the card within their own half – then thoroughly shuffle the cards – and all this while your back is turned. You turn round and instantly find their cards!

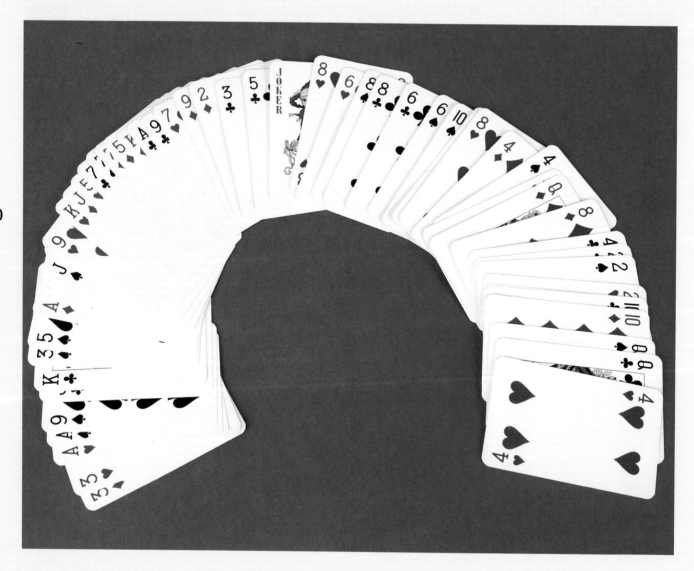

120

1 Pre-arrange the pack beforehand like this: all the odd cards go in the top half (Aces, 3's, 5's, 7's, 9's, Jacks and Kings), and all the even cards go in the bottom half (2's, 4's, 6's, 8's, 10's and Queens). Separate the two halves with the Joker. Put the deck back in the case. You are ready to start.

2 Take the cards out of the case. Spread them to find and remove the Joker. Put it to one side. Give the cards that were above the Joker to one friend and the cards that were below the Joker to the other friend.

3 Tell them to shuffle their cards, then they must take any card from one another's half. They must remember it and then bury it within their own half deck. They must then reshuffle – losing the card that they chose.

121

4 Have each of your friends spread out their cards face upward on the table so that all the cards can be seen.

You have merely to glance at the two spreads to quickly locate the two "strangers" – the odd card in the even group and the even card amongst the odd cards!

Remove both cards and proudly hold them high. Your friends will be astounded!

Note: At the end of the trick quickly gather up all the cards and give them a good shuffle – thus destroying the evidence of your crafty method.

The Two Card Trick

Two cards change places with each other by magic! You try again – they change places once more! Everything can be examined at the end and no-one will be any the wiser.

You will also need a tall hat or a box. The sides should be high enough for you to be able to put cards in and also turn them over without your friend being able to see what you are doing.

1 Take two contrasting cards from your old deck and carefully stick them together – back to back. Double-sided sticky tape is the easiest way to do this, although ordinary glue will do. I use the K♠ and the 2♥.

2 Secretly put the double-faced card in your pocket with the K♠ side facing away from your body. You are ready to start.

3 Remove the regular K♠ and 2♥ from your deck. Show them openly, then drop them into the hat.

Say that you are going to test how observant your friend is.

Tell him that you will remove one card from the hat and put it in your pocket. He must tell you which card is left in the hat.

As if to illustrate how you will do it, you remove the K♠, put it in your pocket where you swap it for the double-faced card which you immediately bring out again with the K♠ side showing.

4 Put the double-faced card into the hat and say that you are now ready to begin the trick.

5 Take the 2♥ out of the hat – show it for a moment – then put it in your pocket.

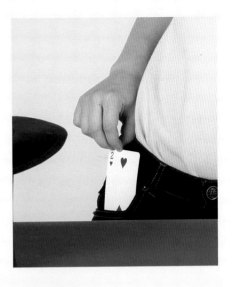

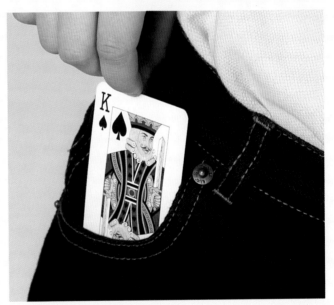

7 Pull the K♠ triumphantly from your pocket!

Offer to do it again. Put both cards in the hat. Turn the double card over and bring it out showing its K♠ side. Put it in your pocket.

What card is left in the hat? The 2♥? No! The 2♥ is in your pocket. Bring out the ungimmicked 2♥ from your pocket. Toss it into the hat.

Let the spectator remove the two cards from the hat and examine everything. It can only be magic!

6 Ask which card is left in the hat. He will say the K♠. Reach into the hat and secretly turn the double card over. Bring it out with the 2♥ side showing, taking care not to expose the other side of the card.

Lazy Aces

This is a gem. With a little practice you can get the spectator to do all the hard work for you while you put your feet up and just direct the proceedings! He finds the four aces and won't have a clue how he did it.

1 Secretly place the four aces on top of the pack and lay the pack on the table.

Tell the spectator that you would like him to do a trick for you.

2 First he must divide the pack into four roughly equal parts. Keep an eye on him and make sure that the quarter with the aces on top ends up in position number 4. If it isn't, casually move it to that position as you apparently tidy up the piles of cards.

3 Tell him to pick up pile number 1 and transfer three cards – one at a time – from the top to the bottom of the packet. He must then deal one card onto the top of the other three piles in any order.

4 You now direct him to put the pile back on the table and pick up pile number 2. Again he should transfer three cards – one at a time – from the top to the bottom of the packet he is holding. Then deal one card on the top of each of the other three piles in any order he wishes before replacing the packet on the table.

You get him to repeat the procedure with piles numbers 3 and 4. The action of doing this to pile number 4 results in you getting rid of the three odd cards that were dumped on it and distributes aces to the top of each pile!

5 Now triumphantly turn over the top card on each pile and watch his face as the four aces appear!

Match of the Day

The shuffled deck is spread face down all over the table. The spectator picks up a card, then you pick up a card. They are now shown and both are red cards. She picks another, you pick one – they are both black cards. You do this a dozen or so times and each time whatever colour she chooses, you manage to match it even though you cannot see the faces of the cards.

1 Before you start, give all the red cards a slight downward squeeze and all the black cards a slight upward squeeze. Now loosely shuffle the two piles together. This should not disturb their distinctive, but almost imperceptible, curves. You are ready to start.

2 Ask the spectator to help you spread the cards out face down all over the table. She will enjoy this.

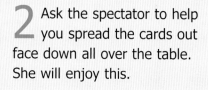

3 Instruct her to drop her finger onto the back of any card she wishes and to drag it towards herself still keeping it face down on the table.

4 The secret curve in the card will be obvious to you.

Go to a different part of the table. Spot a card that is curved the same way as the card that the spectator has just chosen. Drop your finger onto it. Turn your card face up and ask the spectator to do the same with her card. They are both the same colour.

5 Keep doing this. It will be most puzzling to the spectator.

Stop after you have matched up about ten or 12 cards. Gather up all the cards and secretly straighten out the curves so destroying the evidence of the crime!

I "Nose" Your Card

The spectator's card is found – stuck to your nose! This looks very funny!

2 Hold the pack as shown with the faces towards the spectator and your nose pressing on the lower part of the top card.

"What was your card?"

She names it.

1 Get the spectator to choose a card. Secretly look at the bottom card of the deck while she is studying her choice. Remember the card that you saw. Get her to replace her selection on the top of the deck. Cut the pack once to bring your key card directly above her chosen card. Do several more complete cuts apparently to lose her card.

"I am going to find your card in a most unusual way."

As you are saying this, look through the cards and casually cut her chosen card (the one beneath your key card) to the top of the deck.

"I think I 'nose' which card you chose!"

128

3 Keeping your nose pressed onto the back card, slowly lower the hand that is holding the deck. Her chosen card comes into view – stuck to your nose!